LETTER II TO NDI-IGBO IN NIGERIA: UMU-IGBO *QUO VADIS?*

Douglas Nnamdi Egbuonu

M.Litt., M.A., Dip. Pharm

CONTENTS

PREFACE

In the race for life, could a people really be fully prepared for the unexpected and the vicissitudes that could be its lot if things do not go according to plan?

A people who do not have strong leadership and an intrinsic, cohesive unity, tends to disintegrate into disparate parts when faced with any major/serious adversity.

In such ethnic-bound, multi-cultural societies that constitute present-day Nigeria, over the years, Ndi-Igbo have found it extremely difficult to say with certainty who their true friends are, therein. Such frantic and rather inchoate leadership propensity as has been manifested among Ndi-Igbo, in recent days, has seemed to make them all figures of ridicule amongst the other ethnic groups in Nigeria.

Before January 1966, under the fine, sophisticated and articulate leadership of Dr Nnamdi Azikiwe, Ndi-Igbo could boast of true friends in different parts of Nigeria. Faced with the threats of annihilation from the pogroms inflicted upon them in Northern Nigeria in 1966-1967, Ndi-Igbo found truly strong, resilient and dedicated leadership under Dim Odumegwu Ojukwu, and successfully waged a war of survival for up to thirty months. When similarly threatened in 1985/86 with ethnic, religious cleansing by some socio-political and religious fanatics in parts of the North, namely Kano and Kaduna, Ndi-Igbo stood firm and successfully defended their right to reside there and practice their Christian religion freely.

The question that bothers many among Ndi-Igbo today is whether the debacle that befell the Peoples Democratic Party (PDP) in the last 2015 Presidential and States' elections has really so unraveled the confidence of Ndi-Igbo in Nigeria that many among them have given way to unnecessary panic measures, such as are being manifested, by the crisis- precipitating- antics of the Indigenous People of Biafra (IPOB) and/or of MASSOB (Movement for the Actualization of the Sovereign State of Biafra). In politics, as in life generally, a people must of necessity avoid putting all its eggs in one basket.

It is not as if the defeat experienced by the PDP, should not have been expected, after its sixteen years of political dominance, given the level of the poor leadership, governance and performance demonstrated by that party from 1999 till date in 2015. Many Nigerians wanted a change for the better. The APC (All Progressives Congress) posited its hunger and quest to provide a change in governance for the better, and thus, was given a mandate by a preponderant majority of Nigerians to govern, at the Federal Government level and in majority of the States in Northern Nigeria and the South West (S.W.) geo-political zone, including Lagos State.

If Ndi-Igbo had a good, strategic leadership, it would have foreseen the need to recognize the true signs of the times in Nigerian politics, and would have given General Buhari a significant chance to rule as the Nigerian President. Rather, as if blind and deaf, Ndi-Igbo of South East (S.E.) geo-political zone of Nigeria, gave an over-whelming majority of their votes to Dr Goodluck Jonathan, notwithstanding the fact that the latter truly did not do anything significant for the S.E.

Ndi-Igbo must now pause and reconsider. What socio-political grievances do they have against President Buhari? Ndi-Igbo must institute a meaningful dialogue with the new political leadership in Nigeria. Ndi-Igbo should enunciate and present to the President their grievances, as well as a well-articulated programme of the changes they desire, so as to free them from the throes of marginalization, from being treated as second class citizens in Nigeria and their unending frustrations from the bad Federal roads and infra-structures in the S.E. Furthermore, Ndi-Igbo must show that they need Nigeria as much as Nigeria needs them. Indeed, Nigeria needs every socio-cultural group in the country. Many years of being together, living together and plying their trades and professions in different parts of the country, have shown that we all need one another for survival as a nation. Such aspirations and unity of purpose have been abundantly demonstrated whenever our Football teams compete in World or African Continental Football events.

The thrust of this letter, addressed to Ndi-Igbo of Nigeria, is to emphasize that the future of Ndi-Igbo must be articulated and achieved in Nigeria. In this letter, I will look critically and in detail at the questions (or issues) arising from the defeat inflicted on the PDP in the last 2015 Elections: the present predicament of Ndi-Igbo in Nigeria; and the necessary strategic measures to safe-guard Ndi-Igbo in Nigeria.

CHAPTER 1
THE DEBACLE INFLICTED ON THE PEOPLES DEMOCRATIC PARTY (PDP) IN THE LAST 2015 ELECTIONS

The defeat of the PDP by the APC in the last 2015 General Elections has raised many pertinent questions for Ndi-Igbo which call for serious thought and a comprehensive search for correct answers. Some of the issues are:

- Among the ethnic-bound multi-cultural societies that constitute Nigeria, who are the true friends of Ndi-Igbo?

- Has the socio-political pendulum swung fully round again, for Ndi- Igbo, to the 1966–1970 era in Nigeria?

- How do the Ijaws in Rivers and Bayelsa States of Nigeria see themselves, *vis-á- vis* Ndi-Igbo?

- What have been the results of the hijack of the PDP in 1999 by strong forces made up of retired, heavy-weight military men?

- Have Ndi-Igbo achieved reconciliation with the Hausa-Fulani (of the Arewa People) since 1970?

- What about reconciliation with the Middle-Belt peoples of Benue, Plateau, Kogi, Nasarawa, Taraba and Niger States of Nigeria?

- What role does religious affiliation play in the motivation and realisation of true reconciliation between Ndi-Igbo and the Hausa-Fulani (of the Arewa Federation)?

- Don't Ndi-Igbo need a thorough reappraisal of their relationship with the South West (S.W.) States given the unguarded utterances of Oba Akiola of Lagos and the surprising new 'kick in the teeth' dealt them by the Deji of Akure?

I wish to provide answers to each of the above-stated questions, but not in any particular order. My observations and statements will be as fully comprehensive as possible; and are sincere and rational thoughts on the issues at stake. They also could be regarded as starkly dialectical because they are designed to jog our collective minds and wake us up to the need to engage in serious dialogues, intra- and inter-, and to pursue only those objectives that are designed for our collective survival and progress in Nigeria, in harmony, however, with our host communities and environment.

First, among the many socio-cultural nations that make up the country, Nigeria, whom do Ndi-Igbo sincerely regard as their mutual friends? This is not only a tricky question, but also could be regarded as the crux of the problem with Ndi-Igbo in Nigeria. How do Ndi-Igbo's fellow sojourners in Nigeria regard them: as friends or as foes? We, Ndi-Igbo, like the proverbial *Agadi nwanyi*, have stumbled far too many times in Nigeria that, as our collective wisdom dictates, *okwesiri ka aguo ihe nwanyi bu nukpa ya onu* (it becomes necessary that the contents of the old woman's basket should be checked/counted). What have been the pieces of baggage carried by Ndi-Igbo that have tended to cause them to stumble, politically, far too many times?

2

It would not do for our people to argue that the other groups hate Ndi-Igbo because the latter have succeeded in garnering material wealth, educational progress and/or all the other indices that make a people great much more than, say, for example, the Oduduwa peoples of the S.W. geo-political zone of Nigeria. We have also noticed that the Akwa-Ibom peoples of the South South (S.S.) zone of Nigeria, since they were granted their own State, have transformed their State Capital, Uyo, and many other parts of their State in an enviable manner. This is not surprising. Indeed, many of us who had the privilege of attending secondary schools in that State well know how intelligent, hard-working, creative, astute and resourceful they are. What about Lagos State, whose growth in development and wealth by far outstrips the so-called Oil rich States of Rivers, Bayelsa, Delta and Imo? How have Ndi-Igbo States - Enugu, Anambra, Ebonyi, Imo and Abia - performed in comparison with Lagos State?

Given the obstacles through which Ndi-Igbo had to manoeuvre as a result of their losing the civil war objective of living separately in their own country, Biafra, Ndi-Igbo have done very well indeed. However, the other Nigerian socio-cultural peoples have not stood still or idly by. The Oduduwa States of S.W. Nigeria, for example, have excelled above all the other groups in all the indices of development and success, be it in sheer material wealth or in education or in the establishment of strategic infra-structures. Yet, they hardly flout their success in the face of other Nigerians, and thus, tend to become more acceptable generally.

Also, it is true that Ndi-Igbo and the Yoruba have forged quite an abiding relationship, e.g., through inter-ethnic marriages, living amicably and closely together in different local government areas,

3

studying together in institutions of higher education, and even, practicing together in many different professions – medicine, pharmacy, law, *et al*. But, how many of these relationships could be compared with those that had thrived pre-1970, between the likes of Azikiwe and Adeniran Ogunsanya, T. O. S. Benson and Adegoke Adelabu? When compared with their relationships with the Arewa peoples, Ndi-Igbo seemed to have fared very badly. However, the late Emir of Kano, Ado Bayero, remained a life-long, steadfast friend of *Ikemba Nnewi*, Dim Odumegwu Ojukwu. So also was the abiding friendship between K.O. Mbadiwe, Alhaji Abubakar Tafewa Balewa, and Alhaji Zana Bukar Dipcharima.

Second, there seems to have been entrenched this impregnable wall of estrangement between the Arewa and Ndi-Igbo peoples of Nigeria since 1966/67. It does not appear that anything significant has been done or is being done to break down this barrier. Much credit must be paid to President Shehu Shagari for choosing and working so amicably with Dr Ifeanyichukwu Ekwueme as his Vice-President, a partnership that made possible the perfection of the development of the Abuja Federal Capital. That relationship was truncated by another, definitive military incursion into the political governance which foisted General Buhari on Nigeria, as a military dictator. That first advent of Buhari as a military ruler impinged so negatively on Ndi-Igbo's collective psyche and nearly ruined their pace of recovery, post-civil war, through the draconian decrees promulgated by him. Although rescue came through the intervention of General Babangida, followed by General Abacha, Ndi-Igbo elites and businessmen and people in general have not forgotten or forgiven Buhari for the bias he exhibited against Ndi-Igbo generally during his reign, and even afterwards, when again he was crowned by Abacha to manage exclusively the Nigerian Petroleum

4

Trust Fund. Ndi-Igbo have proclaimed their rejection of Buhari with their votes every time he aspired to become the President of Nigeria, including the last Presidential elections of 2015. Having made their statement with their votes, it would not do to dwell on that stance. Ndi-Igbo must move on and send out the Olive branch so as to forge reconciliation through mutual dialogue and respect between them and the Arewa peoples.

Third, the relationship between the Oduduwa and Ndi-Igbo peoples of Nigeria should be allowed to grow, again through mutual respect for one another and active interactions in sports, social life and businesses. It must be emphasized that Ndi-Igbo owe much gratitude to the Oduduwa peoples, especially of the Lagos State, for giving them the opportunity and the living space to survive and succeed in the post-civil war Nigeria.

Ndi-Igbo must continue to show utmost respect and regard for the Oduduwa peoples of the S.W. geo-political zone of Nigeria, notwithstanding the recent, unguarded utterances of Oba Akiola of Lagos and the surprisingly new 'kick in the teeth' dealt them by the Deji of Akure. Ndi-Igbo must carefully weigh their own behaviour and utterances among their host communities in the S.W. They must exhibit all the needed sensibilities and empathy for the norms and mores of their hosts and not fall foul of them and jeopardize the entente cordiale between them. Ndi-Igbo, though, must not bow and scrape, nor exhibit crass servility towards the hierarchical authorities of their host communities. This careful behaviour towards their hosts by Ndi-Igbo notwithstanding, it cannot be right for the Council of Obas in any of the S.W. States to dictate to Ndi-Igbo who their leaders should be in those States.

The Obas should not bar Ndi-Igbo from appointing their own leaders in their domains. Such leaders so appointed, do not compete with the Obas. Rather, they help to ensure that Ndi-Igbo, whom these leaders shepherd, do not fall foul of the Law, and do live and operate their businesses as law-abiding citizens, who also adequately respect constituted authority, especially of the States' governments and the Obas. If the *Eze Igbo* appellation given to the leader of Ndi-Igbo in a particular State is repugnant to the Obas of that State, perhaps Ndi-Igbo should call such a leader *Onyisi* (literally meaning, Leader). In major areas outside *Ala*-Igbo, Ndi-Igbo have always chosen who would lead them as a people, such as the Arewa people have their own leaders whom they call, *Sarikin,* say of Lagos or of Ibadan, as the case may be.

What is required of Ndi-Igbo in any State or area outside Ala-Igbo is to show requisite respect towards the leaders of their host communities, steadfastly minding their own business, and refusing to be tempted into meddling in their politics. Present Nigerian societies, do not as yet respect the country's constitution that clearly affirms that every Nigerian born in any particular State, is an indigene of that State, as well as being a citizen of Nigeria. The moment any Ndi-Igbo 'non-son of the soil' aspires to any political status in any host State (not his/her own so-called State of origin), he or she would fall foul of the political sensibilities of the hosts. This inequality is one of the big shames of present-day Nigeria. It will only disappear, hopefully, in future when Nigerians agree to enthrone the equality and egalitarian rights proclaimed by the country's Constitution.

Meanwhile, Ndi-Igbo who live in Oduduwa land should mind their own business and allow sleeping dogs to lie. After all, what they experience in Oduduwa land of Nigeria is not worse than what they put up with in any of the five different States of the S.E. They cannot even get employment in the state government's civil service where they reside, if the State of origin of their parents is different, even if they could claim to be indigenes of the State by birth. That particular S.E. state would refuse to acknowledge them as true 'sons of the soil'.

Fourth, much more troubling should it be for Ndi-Igbo that they do not seem to have established any significant reconciliation with the peoples of the Benue and Plateau States of Nigeria. Yet, these remain Ndi-Igbo's closest neighbours who share with them many cultural and religious affiliations and practices. Ndi-Igbo have found it hard to forget the fact that they suffered most grievously at their neighbours' hands, during their flights to Eastern Nigeria for safety, during the 1966/67 pogroms in Northern Nigeria and the civil war itself. However, life must go on for Ndi-Igbo and their neighbours. The latter are not fairing any better now than how and what Ndi-Igbo experienced in the past, given the fact of the destruction of human lives and property, these neighbours have been subjected to, owing to the ravaging of their areas by hordes of the Fulani strike force and the Islamic Jihadists. Ndi-Igbo must forgive the past, and endeavour to establish reconciliation with them, through dialogues and mutual understanding and respect. Luckily, prominent personalities from the Benue–Plateau States are still living, who had played active roles in the fights and misunderstandings of the 1966–1970 era. General Yakubu Gowon is alive and has continued to be a prayer warrior for the peaceful salvation of Nigeria. Brigadier-General David Mark has been a prominent Senator (even the Senate President for up to two terms of the PDP hegemony), and has himself forged abiding relationships with many Ndi-Igbo. Ndi-Igbo must, in their own interest, establish peaceful dialogues, with the objective of achieving full

7

reconciliation with its immediate neighbours to the north: the Idoma, the Tivi, Birom, the Jukun, the Igala, the Angas, etc. Ndi-Igbo and they all, have become victims to the expansive ambitions and religious biases of the Arewa peoples. They all could achieve collective protection and peaceful existence, if, through their mutual reconciliation, they agree to live in amity as good neighbours.

Fifth, nearest home to Ndi-Igbo, are the Izom people (the Ijaws) in Rivers, Bayelsa and Delta States, who are indeed their close relatives. It has been asserted that there is scarcely to be found any Ijaw person, especially those of Rivers and Bayelsa States, whose vein does not contain Ndi-Igbo blood .The peoples of the South South (S.S.) geo-political zone of Nigeria were definitely against the Biafran endeavour, and joined forces with the Federal side in the prosecution of the hostilities to drag Ndi-Igbo back into Nigeria, in the 1967–1970 civil war. They have gained tremendously by that strategic political posture and decision, what with their oil wealth and the fact that their zone has produced, before the S.E. zone, an executive President of Nigeria. However, the set-backs they have faced as a result of that strategic, political decision, have been grievous indeed. In terms of gaining stupendous wealth from the Petroleum and Gas, whose great abundance subsists in their zone, they have found to their chagrin that the 'oil-wealth' has indeed benefited the Arewa people much more than they had bargained for, leaving the Ijaws to suffer interminably, without adequate respite or compensation, from the natural disasters that are the hazards and the collaterals of the prospecting and mining of petroleum oil and gas. When their people dared to protest, their leaders were rounded up and executed extra-judicially.

Although Ndi-Igbo have received humiliations and enforced

loss of property and real estate, especially in Port Harcourt, a city that they had contributed enormously in building, pre-civil war, and witnessed their hard-earned real-estates declared 'abandoned property' and gifted more or less *gratis* to the S.S. people; and although many of them (Ndi-Igbo) who were so affected died penniless and heart-broken, and without being adequately compensated, Ndi-Igbo have taken that blow on the chin unscathed and have moved on. We are all witnesses to the fact that the city of Port Harcourt has not, in real terms, developed beyond the stage it had reached as at 1967. Their loss of Port Harcourt, a seaport that previously served the commercial centres of Aba and Onitsha, propelled Ndi-Igbo to focus on the expansion and development of Aba township and market, and instead, actively to use the sea-ports of Warri and Lagos/Apapa to clear their imports, to service the Onitsha and Aba commercial centres.

It is to the credit of Ndi-Igbo that they have not gloated at the throes of the afflicted Ijaws of Rivers and Bayelsa States. These are their closest neighbours and their blood relations. Perhaps, herein lies the sympathy and empathy Ndi-Igbo have exhibited through supporting the political ambitions of the erstwhile President Jonathan and the people of the S.S. zone. However, the crucial question remains: 'how do the Ijaw people of Rivers and Bayelsa States see themselves, *vis-á-vis* Ndi-Igbo of the S.E. Zone?

One can observe, not envy, but a feeling of wonder and surprise at the resilience of Ndi-Igbo. It is also manifest, the guilty feeling they harbour given how they dumped Ndi-Igbo during the latter's trials in the 1967-1970 civil war. One of the prominent S.S. leaders, Ken Sarowiwa, during the meeting held at Hotel Presidential Enugu by the peoples of the erstwhile Eastern Nigeria, comprising the S.E. and S.S.

9

Zones, openly and in tears appealed to Ndi-Igbo to forgive his people and forget their sins of omission and commission against them during the civil war. Alas! for him, that was his last public outing as he was killed extra-judicially, two or three weeks later, for daring to lead his people in protest against the Abacha-led Federal Government of Nigeria.

It does not seem as if there has been a formal treaty of reconciliation and understanding between the Izom peoples and Ndi-Igbo. The Ndi-Igbo adage holds true: *Ogeli bue mmanya bue mmiri omalu nke ka nanyi alo* (i.e., Ogeli soon realizes which is heavier by carrying the palm wine and the water, alternatively). The Izom people have realized that the palm wine (represented by their flirtation with the Arewa people) is a definitely heavier yoke compared with the water, a relatively lighter burden (represented by their age-old relations with Ndi-Igbo). Life must go on between them and Ndi-Igbo. Neither they, nor Ndi-Igbo, can really afford to dwell on the past. Ndi-Igbo and the Izom peoples have continued to intermarry. Port Harcourt has since become again a melting pot for their peoples. One's in-laws can never become one's enemies. Mutual trust and respect must continue to govern their relationship.

Sixth, the political alignments that arose in the wake of Abacha's sudden death and the departure of the military from the governance of Nigeria, gave birth to the PDP in 1999. These were probably aimed at the re-founding of a truly national, democratic movement and a political party open to all Nigerians, from all parts of the country. That was the aim of the founding fathers of the party, until, unfortunately, it was hijacked by strong forces made up of (retired) erstwhile military heavy weights. These financially well-heeled, retired generals, who masquerading as civilian politicians, quickly co-opted retired General Obasanjo, and got him to be chosen as the PDP leader and Presidential candidate, in the aftermath of the departure of the military government, under General Abdusalami Abubakar. That was a move that *ipso facto* dumped Dr Ifeanyichukwu Ekwueme, who was one of the leading lights of the newly formed PDP.

It was conjectured by the strong military men, that the choice of Obasanjo would pour salve on the wound inflicted on the Oduduwa people of the S.W. zone, from the loss of Chief Moshood Abiola, and the stolen June 12 1993 presidential mandate given to him by majority of Nigerian voters. As it has turned out for our country, Nigeria, that co-option of Obasanjo was an unfortunate choice. We all have witnessed the gravity of the lost opportunities that befell the country from that choice.

As usual, in the manner of a people who have failed to learn from its historical past, Ndi-Igbo had wholeheartedly supported the PDP, even though they should have sought alternatives. It should have been obvious to them as a people, that the PDP, as then constituted, had no future for progressive members. Ndi-Igbo have to learn from their historical past; and even though they had wholeheartedly supported the PDP, they should have sought alternatives.

Perhaps, the dogged support Ndi-Igbo have given Goodluck Jonathan could have arisen from their reaction to the forces aligned against him that gave him little chance to articulate his purpose and execute his positive designs for Nigeria. That could have been the strong reason why Ndi-Igbo stood steadfastly by Jonathan. On losing the race to Buhari, Jonathan has demonstrated the marks of a true statesman by conceding defeat without rancour or small mindedness. Therefore, it could be said that Ndi-Igbo's choice of Jonathan has been justified politically and statesman-likely.

11

However, it is not necessary or expedient for Ndi-Igbo to sulk and lick their wounds. They did not vote for President Buhari. That is the fact. Ndi-Igbo should concede defeat such as Jonathan has done, but also should demonstrate that they do not harbour any pathological dislike for Buhari. Life must go on. This should present them with the opportunity to go into close retreat and brain-storming, to choose veritable options for their future political alliances. This, also, should give them the opportunity to reactivate the APGA Party, as a good forum, to bring Ndi-Igbo together in their search for the right political allies from other parts of the country.

Seventh, is the issue of religious affiliation and the role it could play in the motivation and realisation of true reconciliation between Ndi-Igbo and the Hausa-Fulani-Kanuri (of the Arewa Federation). This is a truly tricky and serious question, which needs to be tackled centrally by the Federal and States' governments throughout the country. We, Nigerians, fought a civil war that determined the political future of Nigeria as one indivisible country. We all must uphold and defend the Constitution of Nigeria, which stipulates freedom of religion and worship, and freedom of speech. The upsurge of the Sharia in many States of Northern Nigeria has been the contributory cause of the fanatical jihadist movement in Islam, the extreme manifestation of which we all have witnessed in the murderous deeds of the *Boko Haram*.

The first victims of the killings, bombings and the destruction wrought by the *Boko Haram* were Christians and their Churches. The *Boko Haram* had openly ordered all Ndi-Igbo and Christians to leave Northern Nigeria forthwith. Many Ndi-Igbo have fled the North to escape the mindless killings inflicted on hapless civilians, especially Christians, by the *Boko Haram*. At the beginning of the onslaught wrought by these schismatic Islamists, when the prime victims were Christians, of whom Ndi-Igbo formed the majority, many Muslims in the North remained indifferent. When, however, the *Boko Haram* then began to kill the people in the prime centres of the North indiscriminately, it dawned on many Muslim observers that something had gone hay-wire. It is recalled that when President Jonathan decided to tackle the *Boko Haram* epidemic head-on, and declared a temporary state of emergency in the three most affected North East (N.E.) States of Borno, Yobe and Adamawa, many prominent Arewa leaders, including Professor Ango Abdullahi and the former Inspector General of Police, Coomasie, openly condemned Jonathan and accused him of declaring war on the North. During the early stages of the *Boko Haram* insurgency, even Buhari opined, that the terrorists existed as a figment of fear in the imaginations and the minds of other wary Nigerians. All Nigerians have been witnesses to the narrow escape of Buhari himself, when the *Boko Haram* staged an unsuccessful assassination attempt on him. So also should be recalled the experience of Governor Nyako of Adamawa State, who escaped by the whiskers, when the *Boko Haram* ambushed and attacked his convoy. Did the revered, late Emir of Kano, Ado Bayero not escape narrowly from the murderous raid on him, in his palace, by elements of the *Boko Haram*, who also later on bomb-attacked the Kano Central Mosque? The list of the terror attacks and killings executed by the *Boko Haram* is very long indeed. *Boko Haram* has now earned for itself the nefarious fame of being the most violent, murderous, terrorist movement in the whole world; even worse than the ISIS, by causing the highest number of deaths so far. Can Nigerians ever forget, or come to terms with, the abduction of the over 200 Chibok school girls (most of whom were Christians before their abduction)?

Have we, as a nation, forgotten the notorious exploits of the *Maitatsine* fanatical Sect in Islam in the early 1980s, during the presidency of Shehu Shagari? As long as the Nigerian Supreme Council in Islam, keeps paying lip-service to the need to enshrine and implement true religious freedom, especially throughout Northern Nigeria, as long as many Northern leaders continue to dream dreams of having enthroned an Islamic State in Nigeria, wherein the Sharia law would reign supreme, so long would our country not know peace and religious freedom. If the Supreme Islamic Council in Nigeria is serious, it should work steadfastly to enthrone measures and boards that would ensure that only well-trained, qualified and licensed Islamic religious teachers (i.e., Imams) are accredited and permitted to preach and disseminate the Islamic faith. The Council should sponsor a bill in the National Assembly to prohibit the unqualified and unlicensed dissemination of Islamic faith by preachers who are not licensed and authorized to do so. It must be pointed out that the Christian body in Nigeria has never sponsored, nor allowed, any of its members to wage war against Muslims in the country. Christians have always been victims of the Islamic Jihadists' ravages in many parts of Northern Nigeria.

The question must be asked: why is Islam in S.W. Nigeria so peaceful, progressive and non-violent in contrast to what has been the prevalence of violent Islam in the North? It is a historical fact that Islam reached the South Western parts of Nigeria at about the same time, or period, as it reached the North. Islam has a large following among the Yoruba, but exists peacefully there side-by-side with Christianity. The S.W. Oduduwa children have not allowed either Islam or Christianity to disorientate them from the customs and traditions of their race. Followers of Mohamed in the S.W. are known to marry followers of Jesus Christ and live happily and freely afterwards, to practise their individual religion fully, to the best of their ability and inkling. Christian and Muslim festivals are co-celebrated by members of the same families, without let or hindrance.

Significantly, that has been the probable major reason why Ndi-Igbo have thrived happily in Oduduwa land. Ndi-Igbo are predominantly Christians. Although they did not know Jesus Christ before the advent of Christian missionaries to Ala-Igbo, when they were evangelised by Christian missionaries, Ndi-Igbo could easily embrace the Christian faith because, their ancestor-based religion taught morals and creeds that resembled remarkably the Christian faith and morals. They have in their over-whelming numbers, held on to the Christian faith and practice tenaciously. It could, therefore, be seen the fundamental reason why Ndi-Igbo have gotten on so well with the Yoruba.

Another notable and remarkable fact has been that Oduduwa people successfully fought off the Islamic jihadists who had, indeed, invaded Yoruba-land. After they had lost their capital, the Old Oyo Town, to the invading jihadists, who renamed the town, Ilorin, and had founded a new capital at the new Oyo Town, at its present location, the Yoruba mobilized their united forces and defeated the jihadists, who had essayed to extend their initial conquest southwards. That fact of history could probably, significantly account for the resilience of the Yoruba against imported, violent jihadist Islam. The same could not be averred about the long-lost N.W. Hausa States of, e.g., Sokoto, Daura, Katsina, Kano, Zaria, Bauchi and Gombe; nor about, the N.E. areas won by the El Kaneimi. It is said that Uthman Dan Fodio and the El Kaneimi were contemporaries undergoing Koranic studies in Mecca. It was there, it is believed, that both of them divided Northern Nigeria into the North West and the North East zones, to Uthman Dan Fodio and the El Kaneimi, respectively, as their zones of influence and expansion. Islam was spread throughout those parts of Northern Nigeria by the sword. When the British Colonialists conquered the North, they assured the Emirs that they would protect their areas from any inroads by Christianity. Whatever Animist or native culture and tradition that had existed in the North were swept away by Islam. The people, therefore, do not seem to have any native culture alive today, apart from Islam, unlike what has been the case in the S.W., S.E. and S.S. zones of Nigeria.

The only thing that would save Nigeria from destruction and cleavage, owing to religious/sectarian warfare and violence, is the embracing of, and true respect for, religious freedom and worship. Let nobody ever believe that Ndi-Igbo would allow themselves to be conquered by violent Islamic jihad and/or religious coercion.

CHAPTER 2
PRESENT PREDICAMENT OF NDI-IGBO IN NIGERIA.

With the defeat of the PDP in the last 2015 Presidential and general elections and the consequent grossly one-sided, nepotic appointments made by President Buhari, without due consideration to the federal character representation stipulated by the nation's Constitution, it has suddenly dawned on Ndi-Igbo what a hash they had made by getting themselves, once again isolated, with the inevitable loss of socio-political relevance in Nigeria.

Through the aging, but, still coherent and articulate leadership of the Ohaneze Ndi-Igbo socio-cultural group, President Buhari's attention has been drawn to these obvious mistakes he has so far committed, which have given the impression that he has set out to punish Ndi-Igbo of the S.E. in particular, and the S.S. people generally, who did not give him their votes. In particular, his propensity to appoint his Arewa kinsmen into the most sensitive, strategic posts, and into his core-cabinet, a grievous infringement of the stipulations of the Constitution, has brought out clearly the current marginalisation of Ndi-Igbo.

To my mind, however, President Buhari's determined efforts to curb corruption and to prosecute corrupt officials in the regime of his immediate predecessor, Goodluck Jonathan, is a half-measure and discriminatory, as has been made clear to him by the Ohaneze Ndi-Igbo and other prominent Nigerian leaders. Deeply entrenched corruption in our polity has been in vogue since 1999, and throughout the sixteen years of the PDP hegemony in Nigeria. Personally, what I do object to is the impression given by the incessant rhetoric of some Ohaneze leaders that seems to give the impression that they are holding brief for erstwhile President Jonathan. We cannot afford to be partial and to proffer overt brief and defence for any of the past (PDP) Nigerian Presidents, since 1999.

Corruption has been the great bane of Nigeria and a major cause of the country's failure to become a great and fully developed nation. Having pointed out to President Buhari the need for holistic efforts to probe and extirpate corruption from Nigeria, without fear or favour, Ndi-Igbo's Ohaneze should allow President Buhari to get on with the job. He will eventually be measured by how comprehensively and deeply he has uprooted corruption from Nigeria's polity.

I want to look more closely, though, at the relevant issues raised by the present predicament of Ndi-Igbo in Nigeria, which have caused such disaffection among them that their youths have mounted wide-spread protests throughout the States of the former Eastern Nigeria and the Delta State, egged on by MASSOB (Movement for the Actualisation of the Sovereign State of Biafra) and IPOB (Indigenous People Of Biafra) and its clandestine Radio Biafra (based in London). Ndi-Igbo youths are protesting because, in the first place, their leaders seemed to have betrayed and failed them. Just as nature abhors any vacuum, the Youths have stepped forward and assumed leadership among Ndi-Igbo, which the more mature leaders among them have failed to provide. However, Ndi-Igbo youths seem to be protesting against the effects but not against the cause. We cannot afford to crucify them for making the effort. Rather, the leadership of Ndi-Igbo should now step in and bring sanity into the whole process of agitating for equity and relevance in today's Nigerian socio-political milieu. It does not hold

18

water, the view that the leaders of the MASSOB and IPOB are mere youths; and thus, are not coherent and articulate, or knowledgeable enough. Ndi-Igbo *na si Umu-ibe zim ako na uche* (i.e., the elders among Ndi-Igbo should teach the youths tact and wisdom).

It must always be remembered that the founding Fathers of Nigeria's freedom from British colonialism: Azikiwe, Awolowo, and the Sarduana (Ahmadu Bello), were all young men during the struggle that was waged effectively to gain our nation's Independence. Of course, they were vibrant; they were well motivated; they were enthusiastic the way they mobilized the Nigerian populace in the struggle to gain freedom, from colonial rule and control. Of course, they had mature patrons too, who egged them on and supported their vibrancy and resourcefulness, which only the youth could ensure and assure.

Let me also point out the obvious failure of Ndi-Igbo's leadership in strategic political planning that had resulted in their people putting all their eggs into one basket in the afore-said 2015 elections. Ndi-Igbo similarly did that for Obasanjo. They gave almost all their votes to Yar'Adua; and also to Jonathan in 2011. But they failed in their political reckoning and arithmetic in 2015 when, once again they gave almost all their votes to Jonathan. Some few Ndi-Igbo voices had pointed out in vain the danger of not giving Buhari any chance, Now that Buhari, contrary to his solemn declaration during his swearing in ceremony that he would exhibit the president-for-all-Nigeria posture throughout his presidency, has shown overt political nepotism in his key appointments, his loud body language and utterances, and his rather enigmatic silence to the protests of Ndi-Igbo youths, how would Ndi-Igbo eventually extricate themselves from the consequent political irrelevance, benign neglect and the marginalisation doldrums? However, it is important to point out that many of the grievances Ndi-Igbo have raised against the current Federal Government are antecedent to the advent of President Buhari. These should be attributable to the negligent attention paid during the sixteen years of the PDP governance in Nigeria: to the roads, highways and infrastructures that are in the S.E and S.S. zones of Nigeria. In including these among their complaints, Ndi-Igbo should be careful enough to apportion the blame appropriately. Notwithstanding, President Buhari should consider seriously the redressing of this very bad situation.

Ndi-Igbo need to articulate and provide solutions to the following issues arising from the the last 2015 Presidential and general elections:

- the loss of socio-political relevance;
- the resuscitation of ethnic resentment between Ndi-Igbo and the Arewa people;
- the lack of political focus and dearth of effective leadership among Ndi-Igbo;
- why, forty-five years after January 15 1970, Ndi-Igbo have not achieved true forgiveness and reconciliation with the Hausa-Fulani (of the Arewa parts of Nigeria);
- the re-definition and determination of the Ndi-Igbo Agenda in Nigeria.

i)   The loss of Socio-political Relevance:

It is said that true freedom is never given *gratis*, but must be worked for, fought for and be worthy of being grabbed with both hands. Ndi-Igbo must continue in their efforts to make themselves socio-politically relevant in Nigeria. When any of them is given the privilege to serve, he or she must do so enthusiastically, honestly and effectively. Ndi-Igbo must remain on the part of the solution to Nigeria's problems, economically, politically and socio-culturally. Much reputation has been earned by some Ndi-Igbo who have served their host communities so well, especially in Lagos State. Ndi-Igbo should endeavour to belong to different political parties and play active roles in them. It is not necessary, nor advisable, to crowd into the membership of any ruling political party. Ndi-Igbo really cannot afford to withdraw into their lair and proverbially lick their imagined wounds, just because the political party they had supported in the last crucial elections was defeated. In any race, there must emerge a winner, and at the same time, a loser. What eventually shows the true qualities of an eventual winner (in the long run), is how one, or group, literally pulls himself or itself up to try again and again until success is won. President Buhari is a living example of how one can eventually achieve success after so many defeats and failures.

ii) The Resuscitation of Ethnic Resentment between Ndi-Igbo and the Arewa People:

A more fundamentally disturbing manifestation has been the apparent resuscitation of the ethnic resentment and polemics, between Ndi-Igbo and the Arewa people, that had marked the pogroms on Ndi-Igbo in 1966/67 and the 1967–1970 civil war. In recent times, following the victory of APC over PDP and the emergence of President Buhari, 'another Northerner', there have arisen some rather baiting and unpalatable utterances and polemical verbiage from some notable Arewa sons. It is these postures and utterances, probably, that have provoked the rise of protests and similar polemics from Ndi-Igbo youths in

MASSOB and IPOB. However, at this point in time, one cannot affirm that the utterances of the likes Dr. Muhammed Junaid have the blessing or approval of President Buhari. The real surprise, though, have been the sayings and political postures of prominent Arewa leaders like Professor Ango Abdullahi (former Vice-Chancellor of Ahmadu Bello University, Zaria), and former I.G. of Police, Coomasie , manifested not only during the last National Conference in-house debates, but also, following the victory of APC in the 2015 elections. These highly visible Arewa people are supposed to be very well educated, enlightened and highly respected leaders, not only in the North, but also throughout Nigeria. Although majority of Ndi-Igbo supported Jonathan, it must also be acknowledged that many Arewa people supported him too.

The clearly overt resentment that they have manifested against Ndi-Igbo, came out clearly when President Jonathan decided to prosecute with vigour the war against the *Boko Haram* insurgency by first declaring a state of emergency in the three most affected North Eastern States (of Borno, Yobe and Adamawa). They dared to claim that Jonathan had declared war against the North. They, more or less, denied that there was such a murderous Islamic sect as *Boko Haram*. It was worse when things went badly for the Nigerian Armed Forces in the fight against the above insurgency, especially when the Chibok school girls were abducted by the *Boko Haram*. When Jonathan's and the Nigerian Forces gained any upper-hand in the fight, these Arewa leaders loudly accused the troops of deliberately killing civilians, as if those killed by the *Boko Haram* were soldiers only. These insurgents are terrorists who have gained the notoriety of being the world's most violent destroyers of human lives. In stating the enormity of the resentment and prejudice against Ndi-Igbo shown by these Arewa leaders, one must underline the ethnic typing and profiling that have marked their rhetorics. Jonathan has been called many bad names by these Arewa leaders. The ultimate bad name they seemed to have marked him with, has been that the Bayelsa Ijaw-man Jonathan is an Igbo-man.

It is amazing, one must re-emphasize, that 45 years post-civil war in Nigeria, there still has existed such harbouring and rising expression of antipathy between Ndi-Igbo and the Arewa people. It must, however, be stated again and again, that it was God alone who put us all together into one country. It is the work of God alone that Nigeria has not disintegrated, in spite of the predictions of the country's enemies. Whether it is liked, or not, Ndi-Igbo and the Arewa people will remain: sons and daughters of the same country, Nigeria. Like sons and daughters of one family, we will continue to have our quarrels. But, it behoves us to maintain the future health of our country by finding avenues of true understanding, mutual respect and ceaseless endeavour to maintain honest dialogue between the socio-cultural groups that make up Nigeria. In order to maintain good rapport and useful dialogue between Ndi-Igbo and the Arewa people, two issues, though, must be mutually well-thrashed out in the dialogues: true religious freedom; and, curbing the excesses of the Fulani cattle herders.

Let the Islamic faithful among the Arewa people worship God in accordance with the teachings of their Prophet, Mohammed. Let also Ndi-Igbo Christians worship God according to the Good News (the *Ozioma*) revealed in the Lord Jesus Christ. Let no Sharia intervene to disrupt the peaceful religious equilibrium, provided by the Nigerian Constitution, that does guarantee freedom of religion, freedom of speech and freedom of movement, to all Nigerians.

On the freedom of movement, it must be agreed that, from time immemorial, from the inception of the amalgamation of the Northern and Southern Nigerian Protectorates in 1914, the Fulani cattle herders have had free access to the uncultivated fields of Ala-Igbo in the S.E. and S.S. Nigeria. That has been so until in recent times when there have appeared some Fulani cattle herders who now give the impression that *Ala*-Igbo is a conquered area that rightfully belongs to them for their cattle to graze on indiscriminately, thus destroying cultivated crops. Some communities have protested peacefully, but it does not seem as if the government powers-that-be have listened carefully to their cries and grievances. To underline their power, the cattle herders now flout their strength in their possession of AK-47 automatic rifles which they have been known to use against farmers and villagers who have dared to remonstrate with them for destroying their fields of cultivated crops. Let me not bore the reader with the many recorded complaints of rape and arson committed by these rascally Fulani cattle herders, actions which loudly proclaim that, as victors/conquerors, they have untrammelled rights over the wives and damsels of the conquered people, to say nothing about their cultivated farm crops, as fodder for their beloved cattle.

It is worth noting, that Northern cattle herders have always had the most welcoming hosts in *Ala*-Igbo and by Ndi-Igbo. An insight into what good pasture and security *Ala*-Igbo has always provided them with, could be seen if one motors through Gboko – Katsina Ala – Wukari, during the start of the Rainy Season (in April/May). It would often require that one, in one's vehicle, waits for upwards of 45-60 minutes for the convoy of cattle, on its way towards Adamawa and Yobe States, to cross the Katsina Ala River Bridge, before one could safely cross the bridge too. One would then observe the great number of very young cattle in the convoy that have been born and nurtured in the friendly fields of *Ala*-Igbo during the Dry Season, and before the onset of the Rainy season in April/May of any year. It will eventually be to the loss of the owners of the cattle, if *Ala*-Igbo becomes closed to them as a result of the irresponsible actions of their cattle herders. Something must be done to stop the cavalier and criminal behaviour of the cattle herders before Ndi-Igbo farmers finally lose patience and control of their temper, and collectively decide to take definitive, remedial counter-actions.

iii) The Lack of Political Focus and dearth of effective Leadership among Ndi-Igbo

A pronounced predicament of Ndi-Igbo, in today's Nigeria, is their lack of political focus as a result of the present dearth of effective leadership among them. Many of the former, articulate Ndi-Igbo leaders in the Ohaneze socio-cultural association have openly admitted that they are now too old and tired; and need to encourage the more youthful members to assume the mantle of leadership of the association. This is well and good; but, the younger elements who should rightly assume leadership are badly divided among themselves, and at present, have two factions of the Ohaneze association, each claiming to speak for Ndi-Igbo. At the same time, there is the Youth-wing of Ohaneze singing different songs. There is the MASSOB, whose founder, having inevitably lost his youthful energy and vibrancy, is now quickly turning also into a tired old-man, bereft of fresh ideas. Meanwhile, there has emerged the Nnamdi Kanu-led IPOB with its clandestine 'Radio Biafra' based in London, which has proved a thorn in the flesh of, not only the Nigerian government, but also of MASSOB and the Ohaneze Ndi-Igbo. There is also yet another Ndi-Igbo association called the Aka Ikenga. Its voice does not reverberate, nor does it have the right follower-ship among Ndi-

Igbo. Can these disparate groups and associations be compared with the OPC (Oodua Peoples Congress) and the Afenifere within the S.W. zone, or with the Arewa Consultative Forum and its Youth-wing among the Northerners?

It has to be noted that leadership among Ndi-Igbo should not depend solely on the activities and proclamations of the Ohaneze, or MASSOB, or IPOB. What about the Councils of Ndi-Eze, the Igwes and Elders in S.E. States? What about the Councils of Ezes/Igwes and the Elders of the different Ndi-Igbo communities/towns? Are the usually vibrant Town Unions left in the lurch, un-consulted and not reckoned with? It used to be easy for consensual decisions reached by the different sectors of Ndi-Igbo socio-cultural group to be disseminated to all Ndi-Igbo wherever they may be, and these, to be binding on all Ndi-Igbo.

It is incumbent on all Ndi-Igbo to remain focused and to have, as their governing objectives, the survival and progress of Ndi-Igbo particularly, in Nigeria. This should form the focus of any and every association that aspires to offer and provide leadership to Ndi-Igbo in Nigeria; and in the Diaspora.

Let none among Ndi-Igbo truly believe that *Igbo Enweze*. This is a misnomer and a false principle. *Eze* among Ndi-Igbo does not necessarily mean King as such. What this saying truly signifies is that, although they have acknowledged leaders among them *per se*, Ndi-Igbo do not tolerate dictatorship tendencies in their leaders. Ndi-Igbo are governed most effectively through full and active consultation and dialogue, before a consensual decision is reached, which decision then becomes incumbent on all to accept and fulfil. When an Igwe or Eze of an Ndi-Igbo community begins to govern by dictatorial methods, he invariably, quickly finds himself ignored, if not ostracised by the community. This same tendency permeates every Ndi-Igbo organisation. By nature, Ndi-Igbo are not servile to anybody. They like to be consulted, listened to and their opinion respected by their leaders. When all have had their say in any meeting, a decision is invariably reached by consensus, which decision therefore, becomes binding, on all the members. Thus, the essence of true leadership among Ndi-Igbo rests on full information and consultation of all the members, full and active debate and dialogue, and finally, consensual decisions binding on all the members. Let Ndi-Igbo always remember that that was how our people reached the decision to secede from Nigeria which could no more protect their lives and property; effectively prosecute the thirty months' civil war, and survive all the strictures that the victorious Nigerian Federal Government inflicted on them, post-war.

iv) The Re-Definition and Determination of the Ndi-Igbo Agenda
     in Nigeria:

Let it be loudly proclaimed that Ndi-Igbo truly need the large living space provided by Nigeria, to thrive and effectively make progress in. This implies, all things being equal, that separation from Nigeria should not be a credible option for Ndi-Igbo.

Furthermore, it should be abundantly clear to all sober and right-thinking Ndi-Igbo that the S.E. zone, as presently constituted, with its adverse lack of infra-structures, facilities and opportunities, cannot contain all our people. Moreover, the lack of good infra-structures, industries and resources to provide jobs for many of our educated school leavers, are a great deterrent and repellent to the zone accommodating and sustaining our people.

In addition, Ndi-Igbo should realize that full reconciliation and accord need to be effected between them and their neighbours in North-Central and S.S. zones of Nigeria. Ndi-Igbo should embrace friendly co-existence with all their neighbours, and readily welcome mutual respect and reciprocal recognition with them.

Above all, Ndi-Igbo should learn how to plan in strategic terms, how to play politics effectively, and how to succeed in Nigeria. Ndi-Igbo should consult and dialogue with the S.W. Oduduwa peoples on all crucial matters in Nigeria, and ensure remarkable understanding with them especially in regard to how to institute true Federalism in Nigeria. It has to be pointed out for our education and awareness, that of all the geo-political zones in today's Nigeria, it is only the S.W. Zone which could easily opt out of Nigeria, if pushed to do so, and thrive very well. Otherwise, the way they have structured their own agenda in Nigeria, they will for a long time continue to lead all the other zones in Nigeria in all the indices that show true development and success.

Having considered all the above-stated verities, it becomes important and necessary for Ndi-Igbo to hold seminars and brain-storming sessions to redefine and determine their desired agenda in the Nigeria of today and tomorrow, in order to safeguard Ndi-Igbo in Nigeria. In the third chapter of this work, I intend to suggest some of the elements and strategies that should be considered in determining the 'Necessary strategic measures to safe-guard Ndi-Igbo in Nigeria'.

CHAPTER 3
STRATEGIC MEASURES NECESSARY TO SAFEGUARD NDI-IGBO IN NIGERIA

In this work, in order to bring out and make it more easily comprehended and remembered, I will first of all state the highlights of this chapter and then, where necessary, I will explain in more detail, in subsequent paragraphs, my full thoughts on them. The key strategic measures in this chapter are summarized as follows: Ndi-Igbo should:

- Collectively invest heavily in the education of all their children;

- Concentrate their strategic investments in Ala-Igbo;

- Develop an inland River-port in the S.E. zone;

- Encourage the return of their intellectuals and experts from the Diaspora, even if on Sabbatical basis;

- Invest in building up a strong political party;

- Invest in promoting Igbo Arts and Culture aimed at inculcating into all our people, especially the youth, the essence of good native intelligence, self-respect, self discipline and diplomacy;

- Set up a think-tank for Ndi-Igbo so as to study socio-political and economic issues in Nigeria and proffer dependable solutions to them, on an ongoing basis.

a) Ndi-Igbo should collectively invest heavily in the education of all   their children.

Investment in education of all Ndi-Igbo sons and daughters should be regarded as of fundamental importance, for the progress and

29

survival of all our people in Nigeria. We know that many enlightened Ndi-Igbo parents have made it a priority to get their children well educated to the limit of their individual ability. We recall with gratitude, the sacrifices which many of our parents had made to educate their children properly. Many of our parents had not gone to school because they were forbidden to do so; especially those of them from the more noble families, whose parents had not forgotten, nor forgiven, what the White man did to their culture and civilization when, as colonialists, they seized our land and installed their hegemony over our people. Some more far-sighted parents had not barred their off-springs from 'going to the white man' to get educated (*ije muta akwukwo naka Ndi-Ocha*). When these parents, who had in obedience to their own parents did not get the white man's education, saw how handicapped they had become in making any meaningful progress in the governing system set up by the white man, they swore an oath to give all their off-springs the education which they themselves were deprived of.

It was this whole-hearted quest for education that propelled Ndi-Igbo into the main-stream of progress in Nigeria, in all spheres of human endeavour. But, for the last forty years, Ndi-Igbo have, regrettably, greatly slid down the educational stairs. It was the abundance of educationally endowed Ndi-Igbo that helped many of our people to defeat the evil designs to decimate Ndi-Igbo during the civil war. Ndi-Igbo had many medical doctors and surgeons, many pharmacists and nurses, many scientists and engineers, indeed, many professional men and women, who, by their collective and individual contributions, made our race to survive the civil war relatively unscathed, and begin to thrive again in Nigeria, after January 1970.

It is important for all Ndi-Igbo, to take cognisance of the degradation of the quality of the lives of our people who have failed to get proper, formal education, such as has happened when, after 1970, many of our young people, especially the males, dropped out of schools. Very soon, our people will find they cannot compete effectively in Nigeria, even in modern business ventures and industries.

The kind of deliberate intervention in education needed, as of old by Ndi-Igbo, has to be comprehensive and well thought out. Scholarships and Foundations that offer bursaries should be established and funded at every town community level and by the town unions, the pan-Igbo associations, the Igbo professionals, and by all the wealthy men and women among our people. Educational institutions should be revamped, renovated and expanded to provide enough room to accommodate our children. Many new, qualitatively good secondary and trade schools should be set up to offer adequate instructions to prepare the children for university and other tertiary education, and modern apprentice-ship training, respectively.

Ndi-Igbo should also intervene in university education in particular, by funding the setting up of faculty chairs and modern libraries in all the universities in *Ala*-Igbo, whether owned by the Federal or States' governments; whether set up and run by private individuals or missionaries. Many students' hostels should be built and donated to the higher educational institutions in *Ala*-Igbo.

With these expanded infra-structural facilities and foundations, university faculties should expand the size of their student intakes; and provide adequate room for the increased admission and education of many of our children. Thus, Ndi-Igbo youths would be aroused to aspire to greater heights in education and be equipped, afterwards, for jobs in commerce and industry, and for service in politics and the civil service.

b) Ndi-Igbo should concentrate their Strategic Investments in Ala-Igbo:

It should, by now, be abundantly clear to Ndi-Igbo how very advantageous and wise it is for them to provide all-round industrial and economic development of their own land. The following are key strategic industries: refineries; iron and steel works; pharmaceutical plants; computer and internet technologies; motor spare-parts works; plastic industries; hospital equipment plants, as well as, integrated poultry and agricultural projects, such as have been highlighted in my previous work (cf.: *A Letter to Ndi-Igbo*:... 4.iv 'Agricultural Production', pp. 43 -48).

The benefits that would accrue to *Ala*-Igbo cannot be overemphasized. There would be jobs for our people, especially school leavers – secondary school, trade school and university graduates. The safety of the investments would be better assured. *Ala*-Igbo would be better developed, especially around the cottage industries located in many parts of our land. Ndi-Igbo would be less exposed to hostile host communities. Wealth and foreign investments will pour into the S.E. States because Ndi-Igbo have the population and would be well-to-do enough, to attract these incoming investments. Trade and commerce would increase because traders would come from far and near, in Nigeria and from the neighbouring countries, to buy from our markets.

Ancillary building projects and housing industries would be greatly aggrandized. Storage facilities would be provided through the siting of strategic ware-house facilities. Modern housing estates would be established near the cottage industries, to provide adequate housing for the workers. These building projects would need good investment in electricity generation and distribution.

The up-shot of these strategic investments would transform Ala-Igbo into a rich industrial haven in our own part of Nigeria, without drawing on our people the aforementioned hostility of the people from other parts of Nigeria, where Ndi-Igbo have, hitherto, been helping to open up and develop.

c).   Develop an Inland River-Port in the S.E.:

The industries strategically established in different parts of *Ala-Igbo* would need easier and suitable access to the Atlantic Ocean; seeing, as we all do, that the S.E. zone is land-locked, and has no sea-port of its own. The S.E. has four main rivers that empty into the Atlantic Ocean. These are: Rivers Niger, Ulasi, the Oguta Lake/Sombrero and Imo River. Of the four rivers, the easiest access we have to the Atlantic is through the Oguta Lake and its extension called, the Sombrero River. This is a deep river route that is relatively free from sand banks. If Ndi-Igbo have the mind to establish an inland port to serve their industrial and commercial centres, deep thought should be given to the proposal to construct a deep River-Port on the Oguta Lake, preferably, at Ose Motor. This port will be easily accessible and is centrally located to serve the five S.E. States and, especially, the Aba market in Abia State, the Owerri Industrial Estate in Imo State, the Onitsha and Nnewi markets in Anambra State, and the Emene Industrial Estate in Enugu State. We have seen how bogged down it has been to make the Onitsha River Port, on the River Niger, functional. This project that had been initiated by President Shehu Shagari, has called for the constant dredging of the River Niger, which action has many consequential, deleterious effects on

33

the ecological systems of the riverine communities all along the River Niger to the Niger Delta Area, off the Atlantic. Ulasi River too, may not be suitable given its treacherous under currents and mud-banks all along its journey to the Atlantic Ocean and its mouth at Yenagoa, the capital of Bayelsa State.

If one makes a journey by car towards Port Harcourt from Warri, one could easily identify the above-named rivers as one crosses the bridges over them. It is only the Sombrero River (the river whose source is the Oguta Lake), that one would notice has clear, blue colour showing its deepness, cleanness and remarkable freedom from clogging by sand and mud. Both Rivers Niger and Ulasi (Urashi, among the Ijaws) are deep brown in colour. They carry much sand and mud in them. As for the Imo River, its route to the Atlantic is tortuous; and although it has the deep Owaza Basin that could serve as a river-port, being very near Aba Town and its market, this already is compromised serving, as it has been, as a very large Petroleum/Oil storage depot.

Proof of the suitability of the Oguta Lake and the Sombrero River for the provision of a river-port at the Ose Motor has been shown, when it is recalled too, that it was through the Sombrero River that the Nigerian Naval boats bearing Federal troops came all the way from Rivers State to capture, for a brief period in 1968, the Uli Airport, which had served Biafra as its sole gateway from and into Biafra during the hostilities. We recall, of course, how fierce the battle was, that enabled Biafra to destroy that expeditionary incursion. Ships and barges can move more easily and sail up to Ose Motor on Oguta Lake, if the S.E. States could invest into making the provision of this important river port a reality.

Of course, we are aware that Sea Ports and River Ports, like

Airports, do fall under the responsibility of the Nigerian Federal Government. However, States could participate in the development of such strategic river ports as is being suggested in this work. We do recall how Governor Sam Mbakwe's Imo State, single-handedly, built the Airport in Imo State whose management was taken over by the Federal Government.

    d).   Encourage the Return of Ndi-Igbo Intellectuals in the Diaspora:

    The intellectual wealth belonging to Ndi-Igbo race that is outside Nigeria is enormous. The return of a good number of these intellectuals is *sine qua non*; especially, when we consider the great input they could make to perfect and actualise the above strategies, numbers a) through c), already considered in this chapter. Ndi-Igbo intellectuals in the Diaspora would be greatly needed in the education of our children. They would be invaluable in, especially, the implementation of the suggested industrial revolution of Ala-Igbo, to say nothing about their knowledgeable inputs in the engineering design and construction of the River Port at Ose Motor on Oguta Lake; and the refineries for petroleum products. Ndi-Igbo intellectuals, except those who personally choose to return home permanently, could be encouraged to come home on sabbaticals and then go back to their jobs abroad, at the end of the specific assignments they have elected to do at home.

e).   Ndi-Igbo should build up a strong Political Party and Alliances:

Ndi-Igbo should take part in building a strong political party and alliance that would be attractive to the generality of the S.E. and S.S. States (including Delta State). The peoples of the former Eastern Region and Mid-West Region have had centuries of socio-cultural and religious linkages and contact.

This political party or alliance could be as a starting point, towards founding further alliances with like-minded politicians from the Edo and S.W. States, as well as the Northern States. It should not be an omnibus type political party, made up of disparate people, that has no strong ideological structure or unity. The kind of political party envisaged should have a well-reasoned and articulated manifesto and philosophy, which should attract like-minded and serious Nigerians, who are honest and well-motivated by the urge and determination to serve their fellow citizens, and build up the country into a true nation.

The political party should not be a safe haven for corrupt money-bags. It should welcome only those Nigerians who truly and sincerely love the country and would, at all times, defend the Constitution so as to turn Nigeria into a free democratic nation which assures all her citizens freedom of religion, freedom of speech and association, freedom of life itself; and above all, a country that values the sacredness of human life.

In fact, if our people are serious, they would not see some of the above-stated objectives of the political party as being utopian, but as achievable, so as to evolve an egalitarian society which encourages each of its fellow-citizens to aspire to attain the stars, if given the opportunity.

f).   Invest in the Promotion of Igbo Arts and Culture:

The promotion of Igbo Arts and Culture should be something which is very special to all Ndi-Igbo people. We all are products of Igbo culture and tradition, and all whose very lives and beings manifest the best that the Ndi-Igbo socio-cultural attributes endow: to stand tall and distinct even in any crowd.

Chapter 3 of my previous work, *A letter to Ndi-Igbo: Needed,*

Edifying and Crucial Attributes, has highlighted comprehensively the need for the socio-economic revival of Ndi-Igbo. It also called for the cultural renaissance among Ndi-Igbo; the revival of Igbo Language, the vessel of Igbo culture; keeping Igbo culture sacrosanct as well as dynamic; and for making Ndi-Igbo society truly inclusive. Except for making appropriate references to and from the above work and its chapter 3, the current follow-up missive will dwell more on what needs to be done so as to invest well in the promotion of Igbo Arts and Culture.

As I had stated in my first letter to Ndi-Igbo, 'it is important to take pains to retain and propagate among Ndi-Igbo all those qualities that make Igbo people distinct, unique and notable. These attributes are usually found in the language, legends and the liturgy of the people ...', (ibid. p. 15). One of the requirements for the renaissance of Igbo Arts and Culture is the availability and selection of prominent personalities among Ndi-Igbo who should become Patrons of Igbo Arts and Culture. These Patrons should be drawn from the following personalities: teachers (in the primary and secondary schools); university dons (especially, from the Arts and Humanities faculties); State Governors; Chairmen of Local Government Councils; Ndi-Eze/Igwes and Nze-na-Ozo; Chairmen/ Presidents of Town Unions; the 'Eze Igbos' (or the *Onyisis*) in non-Igbo areas; and other Leaders of Thought. These Patrons are necessary to motivate, support financially and morally, the propagation of Igbo Arts and Culture.

The prior mobilisation of the youth and women is a fundamental requirement for the success of this investment, for they indeed, form the vehicle and are the real propagators of Igbo culture. Also, it is important to define correctly what should constitute the ingredients of the Igbo Arts and Culture. I reckon that emphasis on dance, music, arts and crafts, Igbo Language, expositions on the Igbo custom and tradition, should comprise the Arts and Culture that we should aim at promoting.

The classification of the constituents of Igbo Arts and Culture should break these down into:

- Artefacts –Metal/Bronze, Wood Carvings: masks, doors/gates, chairs (e,g, *Oche Mpata*), Paintings and Murals – using *ufie, uli* and/or *nzu* ;

- Songs and Music – e.g., Gospel Songs/Music; Songs connected with dances – e.g., *Egedege; High-life; Egwu Oja; Igba Eze; Igba Ijelle*, etc, and Songs connected with funerals, marriage ceremonies; outing ceremonies in connection with New-born Babies, etc.

- Beautification of landscapes/environment; Events' Halls; erection of Sculptures of Ndi-Igbo Heroes; creation of Halls of Fame to honour and immortalize Ndi-Igbo Heroes; creation of Departments of Culture and Tradition in the State's Ministry of Culture and Tourism. In this endeavour, the efforts of Governor Emeka Omerua, of blessed memory, to add beauty to Ala-Igbo environment should be fondly remembered.

The primary requirement for the propagation of Igbo Arts and Culture is that of deliberately teaching all Igbo children the Igbo Language. To be effective, this should not be left to the parents alone. Literacy and fluency (oral and written) in Igbo Language should be taught as a matter of fundamental policy, in all nursery and primary schools, as well as in the junior secondary schools. The fact cannot be gainsaid that Igbo Language is, and should be, the veritable vessel and medium of Igbo Culture. Solid foundation for this very important requirement should be laid early in the lives of our children. As I had emphasized in my earlier work, 'it should be the fundamental policy of

State Governments in S.E. Nigeria to make Igbo Language the compulsory medium of instruction in the early years of our children's education in all schools, public and .private alike' (see, *Letter to Ndi-Igbo* ..., pp. 23-24).

Igbo dance and music are greatly integrated in the Igbo Language. A careful listener and observer would notice that the flutist, say, in the dance of damsels, for example, calls out the tunes and dance choreography in special and fluent, descriptive Igbo slangs, which could be intelligible only to those who are initiated through practice. Also, it is the big gong which directs the intensity of the dance tune and the dancing. The expert flutist sings beautifully in Igbo Language as he inspires, motivates and urges the dancers to greater efforts. An Igbo child, who is tone deaf to, and dumb in Igbo Language, would stand out like a sore thumb if he/she tries to dance with all other boys and girls who speak and understand the Igbo language fluently.

A veritable way of propagating Igbo Arts and Culture could be to organise Cultural Fairs and Arts and Dance competitions among different Igbo communities, at both the local government and State government levels. Another way is to stage inter-State Cultural Exchanges with neighbouring States and with Ndi-Igbo in the Diaspora. Ndi-Igbo who reside and do business in non-Igbo States should regularly bring out different famous Masquerades and Dance Troupes as part of joining in major celebrations of their host communities, e.g., during a prominent festival such as the outing ceremony of a newly crowned Obi, or to mark prominent general festivals, e.g., Christmas, Independence Celebration, the New Yam Festival, etc.

To all those attributes which bring out luminously and attractively the culture of Ndi-Igbo must be added the need to inculcate in all our people, from their very young age, the need for good native sense and intelligence, modesty, self-respect, self-discipline and diplomacy. Ndi-Igbo should be taught especially to be diplomatic, self-discerning and self-disciplined in their life-style, and in particular, in all their dealings with other Nigerians. When to the innate good inheritance of every Igbo son and daughter is added good up-bringing, taught at home and in the schools of life, invariably the model of behaviour of the young boys and girls would be improved and last them throughout their lives.

It is true that each of us is a product of our own culture and education. Any culture that does not provide as its end product an all round civilized human being should be looked at seriously again and again. A people cannot afford to justify, through its stiff-necked-ness, the bad name and insult cast on it by its opponents (i.e., *Okwesighi ka mmadu di ka onu akoroya ako*). It is important that in propagating the Arts and Culture of Ndi-Igbo, all those abrasive characteristics of the average *Nwa*-Igbo be corrected and erased from them. How well this is achieved would greatly edify Ndi-Igbo socio-culturally.

May I be allowed to present in conclusion of this sub-section of chapter 3, the following nugget of wisdom from C.S Lewis, *Miracles: A preliminary Study* (p. 53):

"A society where the simple many obey the few seers can live;
  a society where all were seers could live even more fully.
  But a society where the mass is still simple and the seers
  are no longer attended to can achieve only superficiality,
  baseness, ugliness, and in the end extinction."

g).   Set-up An Ndi-Igbo Think-Tank (or Study Group):

The main objectives of this Think-Tank would be to study closely the socio-political and economic issues that arise in Nigeria and to proffer/recommend dependable solutions to them, on an on-going basis. The members of this study group should not be the mouth-piece of Ndi-Igbo. The recommendations proffered by the study group should be addressed to Ndi-Igbo Leaders, namely, Ohaneze Ndi-Igbo, the S.E. States' Governors, and current members of the National Assemblies (the Senate and the Federal House of Representatives). Ndi-Igbo must speak with one voice. When other highly placed Nigerians denigrate and rain abuses on Ndi-Igbo, they should be answered, not by all and sundry Ndi-Igbo, but only by well-reasoned responses by the Leadership of the pan-Igbo people, and not in an *ad hoc* manner or by abusive polemics.

I would suggest too that the membership of the standing Ndi-Igbo Think Tank should not exceed 25, made up 5 members from each of the five S.E. States. The members should be drawn from the religious bodies, the universities, renowned professionals, the industry, revered statesmen and women, and seasoned politicians.

The need for the standing Ndi-Igbo Think Tank has been long over-due. When constituted and inaugurated, under the auspices of the five States' Governors, the Think Tank should form key committees that would embrace and study the different aspects of the socio-political and economic issues that exist in Nigeria. The findings and recommendations by the committees should be considered and approved by the full Think Tank body, before they are reported to the authorities that set it up, as per the above-stated suggestions. For Ndi-Igbo, the Think Tank is a long-needed idea whose time has now dawned in present-day Nigeria.

EPILOGUE

Eventually, it is the extent and depth of the development wrought by Ndi-Igbo in Nigeria, preferably in *Ala*-Igbo, which will preserve them and give them the respect and regard they merit. Ndi-Igbo should not wait on the Federal Government of Nigeria to extend any largesse to them, or to the S.E. zone of Nigeria, for that has never been their lot from the beginning of Nigeria's nation-hood.

When after many petitions and requests from the Eastern Nigeria Region, the Tafawa Balewa-led Federal Government of Nigeria decided to build the bridge across River Niger to link Asaba to Onitsha, the West to the East of Nigeria, did not the federal government proclaim that bridge the first toll-gate infrastructure in Nigeria? That toll-gate was sited at the Asaba end of the bridge to make sure our people paid the toll without demur. When a similar road bridge over River Niger at Jebba was completed, no tolls were collected from the people who were mostly served by the Jebba Bridge (which linked Northern Nigeria to the West and Lagos). Ndi-Igbo opted to pay the toll rather than continue to undergo the trauma of crossing from Asaba to Onitsha and vice versa, using the unreliable pontoons. The Asaba-Onitsha Niger Bridge was badly damaged during the civil war, and needed to be reconstructed at the end of the hostilities, in 1970. Curiously, as soon as its reconstruction was completed and it could be in use again, the toll-gate at the Asaba end went into operation once more until the Federal Government reckoned that our people had completed the repayment of the investment incurred in building the bridge in the first place, and the reconstruction of and the repairs on the bridge after the civil war.

Ndi-Igbo could understand the rationale behind the collection of tolls from all users of the newly constructed infra-structure such as the bridge over River Niger linking Onitsha to Asaba. But, that business-like decision should have been immediately applicable to all subsequent, strategic infra-structures built by the same Federal Government, such as, e.g., the Jebba Bridge. Such decisions should be holistic so as to be fair to all sections of the country, just as the Federal Government rather belatedly decided to institute the utilisation of toll-gates on all its highways and major bridges many years afterwards.

In fact, Ndi-Igbo could understand, and make allowance, for the fact that no development wrought in Ala-Igbo by the Federal Government of Nigeria could ever be given *gratis*. When General Buhari was asked, during his first advent as a military dictator/ruler of Nigeria, why little was being done by the Federal Government, to help Ndi-Igbo States recover fully after the devastation of Ala-Igbo during the civil war, he blurted out a thought-provoking statement. He stated, *inter alia,* that anybody who passed through the Onitsha metropolis in the 1980s could hardly believe that that was the same Onitsha which had been grievously devastated during the civil war. The extent of the renovation and development of the town, clearly manifested to the observer, would prove that Ndi-Igbo did not require any further help, or input, from the Federal Government. In fact, he clearly believed that Ndi-Igbo should get on as best they could, without any help from the central government of Nigeria.

What General Buhari refused to believe was that the recovery efforts by Ndi-Igbo, to revamp their economic status and reconstruct the infra-structures in *Ala*-Igbo, were all due to the self-efforts by individual *Umu*-Igbo. The Federal roads through *Ala*-Igbo were in tatters and decrepit – full of ruts and deep pot-holes. Yet, Ndi-Igbo taxed themselves to provide adequate housing for themselves and their people.

The East Central State Government, under Ukpabi Asika, did not reconstruct the houses damaged by the civil war. That government got back from the Onitsha Market traders, every penny that was spent in re-building the Onitsha Main Market, which had been completely burnt down during the civil war. It must be re-emphasized, that individual Ndi-Igbo rebuilt their damaged houses and constructed new houses to provide accommodation for the populace in the townships of Onitsha, Aba, Enugu, Abakaliki, Owerri, Awka and Nnewi, etc.

It is crystal clear, therefore, to Ndi-Igbo, that true development is rather acquired through pains-taking study, emulation and practice. Rather than continuing the attempt to bring about the desired development of Ala-Igbo, through uncoordinated, individual efforts, Ndi-Igbo should go about installing the development of *Ala*-Igbo, by strategic group efforts, aimed at achieving set-goals and objectives. This could be a key function of the suggested 'Think Tank' for Ndi-Igbo. It should also be clear, to all, that steadfast development is a gradual and evolutionary process with set-objectives, goals and time-tables.

It is important that we all should understand and accept that the development of *Ala*-Igbo will affect our own children, grand-children and the future generation, and help to stop the massive escape of our children to the greener pastures abroad, to the more developed countries, outside Nigeria. When fully in place, the development will wipe away tears from our frustrated children, marginalised, discriminated against and unemployed as thousands of them are in present-day Nigeria. The development will add more grease to the elbows of *Umu*-Igbo children, and stimulate their innate enthusiastic resourcefulness, and awaken, by the same, their creative capacity, for collective and individual advancement.

44

Another important ingredient of good development is that it is communal in context. Individuals could provide the impetus, but a careful look at those developments that have lasted pretty long in Ala-Igbo would show that they have been achieved by communal efforts, and been inspired and motivated by good governance. It is remembered how the Michael Okpara-led Eastern Nigeria Regional Government provided the matching grants, that catalysed and motivated communities in *Ala-Igbo*, to complete development projects, such as, the building/equipping of schools, and general hospitals; the provision of potable water for entire communities, and even the construction of rural roads, etc.

In this study, emphasis has been placed on steadfast developments which are the product of sound strategic planning and disciplined implementation. The 'Think Tank', the State Governments, the enlightened entrepreneurs of the private sector, and Ndi-Igbo communities should all take part to ensure that the desired developments, envisaged by this work are not haphazard, ragged or un-co-ordinated.

www.ingramcontent.com/pod-product-compliance
Lightning Source LLC
Chambersburg PA
CBHW071250280526
45788CB00004B/1661